Florida A to Z

Florida

PINEAPPLE PRESS, INC. SARASOTA, FLORIDA

A to Z

Susan Jane Ryan

illustrated by
Carol Tornatore

Copyright © 2003 by Susan Jane Ryan and Carol Tornatore

Inquiries should be made to:
Pineapple Press, Inc.
P.O. Box 3889
Sarasota, FL 34230

www.pineapplepress.com

Designed by Carol Tornatore

Library of Congress Cataloging-in-Publication Data
Ryan, Susan Jane.
        Florida A to Z / Susan Jane Ryan ; illustrated by Carol Tornatore.—1st ed.
                p.   cm.
        Summary: Reveals Florida's people, places, animals, history, and other
characteristics through a collection of brief descriptions for each letter of the alphabet.
        ISBN 1-56164-249-5 (alk. paper)
1. Florida—Juvenile literature. 2. English language—Alphabet—Juvenile literature.
        [1. Florida. 2. Alphabet.] I. Tornatore, Carol, ill. II. Title.

        F311.3 .R93 2003
        975.9—dc21

                                                                            2001052092

First Edition
10 9 8 7 6 5 4 3 2 1

Printed in China

In loving memory of my mother, Florence Rosch Leibick,
a brave adventurer, who, upon crossing into Florida
for the very first time, stopped at a restaurant for breakfast
and asked the waitress, "What's a grit?"

Susan Jane Ryan

For my children and grandchildren
—with love

Carol Tornatore

Florida
A to Z

A

Cannonball Adderley

Born in Tampa in 1928, Cannonball Adderley, was a famous jazz alto saxophone player. His real name was Julian, but friends called him Cannibal because of his enthusiastic eating habits. This nickname was later changed to Cannonball. Adderley played with the Miles Davis Quintet until he formed his own jazz band in 1959.

Apalachicola

In 1836, the Apalachicola River was used to transport bales of cotton to market. The city of Apalachicola became the third largest cotton port on the Gulf Coast after New Orleans and Mobile, Alabama. The cotton was shipped to Columbus, Georgia, and eventually made its way to New England, England, France, and Belgium. Cotton mills and lace manufacturing centers were the final destinations of the cotton grown in the area. Present-day Apalachicola is famous for its succulent oysters rather than cotton.

Atlantic Sailfish

What makes this fish special is its long, pointed bill and incredible sail-like dorsal fin. The sailfish can reach 10 feet in length. When it is hooked, it leaps high into the air and appears to be walking on its tail on the water. It gyrates its entire body and whips its head from side to side. In 1975, the state legislature adopted the Atlantic Sailfish as the state's official saltwater fish.

Aquifer

The Floridan Aquifer is a naturally occurring underground water reservoir that spans 82,000 square miles. Most potable—or drinkable—water can be found within 50 to 200 meters below the surface. The water in the aquifer comes from rainwater that seeps through the soil and limestone. This process is called recharge. When the amount of water removed from the aquifer through springs or wells is greater than the recharge amount, the aquifer level goes down.

9

Audubon House

John James Audubon lived in this mansion while painting beautiful and accurate portraits of Florida wildlife and birds. The owner of the clapboard house, a sea captain, salvaged many of the antiques used to furnish the house from ships that sank off the coast. The Audubon House and Gardens, an interesting tourist destination, is located in Key West.

Agriculture

The state of Florida is comprised of 35 million acres. Ten million of these acres are used to produce more than 35 billion pounds of food per year. Florida is the number one citrus-producing state in the nation. It ranks second in vegetable production and fourth in all crops. Forty thousand commercial farmers make their living in the state of Florida.

Alligator

One of the largest alligators ever found in the state measured 13 feet 10 inches and weighed 1,043 pounds! An alligator may eat 150 – 200 pounds of food a day. This hefty diet consists of fish, frogs, birds, and snakes. Large male gators have been known to eat raccoons, wading birds, small pet dogs, and even cows. The powerful jaws of an alligator are strong enough to crack cattle bones, but once the jaws are shut, they can easily be held closed with bare hands.

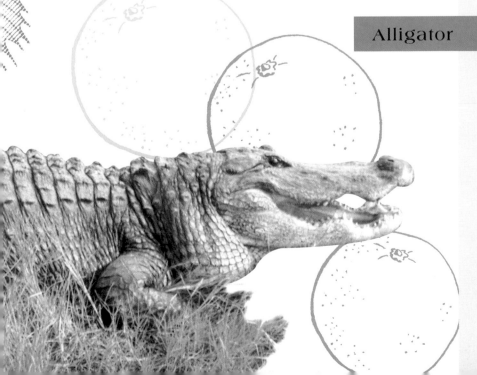

Busch Gardens

Busch Gardens is a 335-acre family fun park located in Tampa. It boasts the largest and fastest roller coaster in the Southeast United States, the Kumba. It also has one of the top zoos in the country, with almost 3,400 animals.

Barefoot Mailman

In 1885, there were no roads or railroads connecting Palm City (present-day Palm Beach) to Lemon City (Miami). The early settlers had to get their mail somehow. So the U.S. Postal Service created a round-trip route of 136 miles along the untamed coastline. This difficult journey consisted of 80 miles by foot and 56 miles by boat! The men who carried mail on this route walked the beaches barefoot most of the way and used a small boat to cross the Hillsboro Inlet. Each of these men became known as a "Barefoot Mailman." The first road from Lemon City to Lantana was built in 1892, the last year the Barefoot Mailman traveled his route.

POSTMARK AMERICA

Mary McLeod Bethune (1875–1955)

A child of former slaves, Mary McLeod Bethune spent her life fighting for the right to education and freedom from discrimination for African Americans in the United States. Bethune started a school for Negro girls in 1904 in Daytona Beach. Eventually this school grew to become a high school, then a junior college, and finally Bethune-Cookman College.

Bats

The most common bat in Florida is the Mexican free-tailed bat. These furry mammals eat thousands of insects each night. Free-tailed bat colonies can number from 50 to over 20,000 bats. Strong fliers, they can zoom as fast as 60 mph and fly as high as 2 miles.

Bok Tower Gardens

The beautiful Bok Singing Tower in Lake Wales is surrounded by lush gardens and wooded pathways. The tower and gardens were a gift to the American people from Edward Bok, an editor and Pulitzer Prize–winning author. Every afternoon there is a live concert from the 60-bell carillon in the tower. You can hear the bells ringing for miles.

Chief Billy Bowlegs

At the end of the Second Seminole War in 1852, a few hundred Native Americans fled to the Everglades and the Big Cypress Swamp. When soldiers began to harass his village, Chief Billy Bowlegs led his people in the Third Seminole War. The war lasted from 1855 – 1861, when most of the remaining Seminoles were sent to live on a reservation in Oklahoma.

Beaches

Sandy beaches make up more than 1,000 miles of the Atlantic Ocean and Gulf of Mexico coastlines along Florida. Florida's beaches are consistently ranked as some of the best in the United States.

Coreopsis

Florida's official wildflower is the colorful coreopsis. This tall, yellow flower, which resembles a black-eyed Susan, is found in every county in Florida. The flower is a food for seed-eating birds, as well as a natural dye that produces a vivid orange color.

Castillo de San Marcos, Coquina, and Coacoochee

The Castillo de San Marcos, a Spanish fort, was built in St. Augustine between 1672 and 1695. The walls of the fort were built primarily from coquina, a sedimentary rock formed from pieces of shells, tiny fossils, and limestone. During the Seminole Wars, the great chief Coacoochee was held in the small jail in the fort. He starved himself until he was thin enough to slip through the bars on a window and escape. Coacoochee became one of the most respected Seminole chiefs after the death of Osceola.

coquina

Cross and Sword

The Official State Play of Florida tells the story of the European colonization of St. Augustine, the oldest permanent settlement in North America. The play is presented during the summer months under the stars in an open-air amphitheater located in St. Augustine. Pictured above is Chief Oriba of the Timucuans, who confronted Menéndez when he founded St. Augustine in 1565.

Cypress Tree

In the early 1900s, cypress trees—some over 800 years old—were harvested for their decay-resistant heartwood. This valuable wood was used in the building industry for shingles, paneling, and decking. Although the majority of these majestic, old-growth trees were cut down, the largest cypress tree in Florida, the Senator, still stands in Big Tree Park outside Longwood.

Calusa Indians

The Calusa Indians lived in southwest Florida along the shores of the Gulf of Mexico from Tampa Bay south to Cape Sable. This extinct ancient tribe of Native Americans lived off the ocean and its bounty. They ate fish and shellfish and used fish bones and seashells to make weapons and tools. They traveled in dugout canoes. In 1896, Frank Hamilton Cushing excavated a Calusa Indian site on Key Marco and unearthed many beautiful animal carvings and other artifacts.

Cross-Florida Barge Canal

The idea of a canal that crossed the state of Florida, linking the Gulf of Mexico with the Atlantic Ocean, had been around for hundreds of years. In 1933, the Canal Authority was created to build a cross-state canal. During the 38 years—from the project's beginning to its end— $70 million was spent and the Cross-Florida Barge Canal was one-third completed. In 1990, the 110-mile corridor of land originally intended for the canal was designated as a greenway for conservation and recreation.

Cypress Gardens

Cypress Gardens—Florida's first theme park—is a 200-acre floral wonderland located in Winter Haven. It is noted for its famous water-skiing shows, Southern belles, and magnificent gardens.

Dolphin

The Atlantic bottlenose dolphin is the state saltwater mammal. Also known as a porpoise, it is the most common dolphin found in the shallow coastal waters off Florida. This playful, friendly creature has been known to follow boats and frolic with humans in the warm waters surrounding Florida.

Hernando de Soto

Hernando de Soto was a famous Spanish conquistador who was sent by the king of Spain to find gold in the new world. He landed in Tampa Bay in 1539 to begin one of the first major explorations of the southern part of North America. His explorations took him through northern and western Florida. De Soto never found gold.

Marjory Stoneman Douglas

A famous writer and environmentalist, Marjory Stoneman Douglas lived in a small cottage in Coconut Grove for the last 70 of her 108 years. She wrote The Everglades: River of Grass, which sparked interest in saving this unique ecosystem. Through her conservation efforts, Everglades National Park was established. She also founded an organization called Friends of the Everglades. In 1997, a 1.5-million-acre wilderness area in the Everglades was dedicated in her honor.

Daytona International Speedway

The Daytona International Speedway is home to the famous Daytona 500 sports car race. The winner of the first Daytona 500 in 1959 was Lee Petty, beating Johnny Beauchamp by a mere two feet. One loop around the track is 2.5 miles long.

Fort Jefferson in the Dry Tortugas

Dry Tortugas

The Dry Tortugas are the last seven reef islands in the string of keys that extend west from Key West into the Gulf of Mexico. They were named by Ponce de León after the tortoises that he found living there (*tortuga* is the Spanish name for turtle). Fort Jefferson, the largest masonry fort in America, was built on Garden Key. Samuel Mudd, the doctor who set John Wilkes Booth's leg, was imprisoned at Fort Jefferson for complicity, or helping, in the assassination of Abraham Lincoln. The fort and the islands became a national monument in 1992.

Diving

Exploring underwater Florida can be a fascinating pastime for natives and tourists alike. Scuba divers love to discover the amazing marine plants and animals that live in the coral reefs off the Keys. Archaeologists are excited by the Native American artifacts and fossils that can be found in the many springs and underwater caverns located throughout the state.

Eagle

Our national bird, the bald eagle, is found in every state in the Union except Hawaii. Florida has nearly twice as much eagle nesting territory as any other Southern state. The bald eagle has a wingspan of up to 90 inches and can weigh up to 15 pounds. This fish-eating bird lives near large bodies of water and nests high in tall trees. A threatened species, the bald eagle mates for life and produces 1 to 3 eggs per year.

Egrets

One of the most abundant egrets found in Florida is the cattle egret. These white birds are often seen in pastures, perched on the backs of cows or trailing behind them, eating the insects that have been uncovered by the cows' hooves. Cattle egrets, which are native to Africa, were helped across the Atlantic by strong tailwinds sometime during the 1950s.

Everglades National Park

Located at the southern tip of the Florida peninsula, it was established in 1947. This 1.5 million-acre preserve is the largest subtropical wilderness in the United States. A fragile eco-system and natural biological wonder that harbors many endangered species, the Everglades is threatened by the diversion of water to populated areas of south Florida, by pollution, and by invasive nonnative plant species. Efforts are now under way to restore the Everglades.

16

Eglin Air Force Base

Eglin Air Force Base, located near Valparaiso, Florida, is one of the largest bases in the world. It consists of 724 square miles of land ranges and more than 86,500 square miles of water ranges. In 1941, Eglin became a training site for Army Air Force fighter pilots. Jimmy Doolittle, a famous WW II fighter pilot, trained his B-25 crew for their raid against Tokyo at Eglin Air Force Base.

Gloria Estefan

Gloria Estefan was born in Cuba in 1957 and fled with her family to Miami in 1959 to escape political persecution. While a university student, Gloria joined the band that would become The Miami Sound Machine. Their 1985 hit "Conga!" is the only song in U.S. history to appear on Billboard's Pop, Latin, Soul, and Dance charts all at the same time. In 1989 Gloria Estefan released her first solo album. Today she is one of the most successul and well-loved singers in Florida and around the world.

Estuaries

An estuary is located where fresh water combines with salt water, specifically where a freshwater river meets the ocean. Estuaries abound with a large diversity of fish, birds, and other wildlife. These sheltered waters are protected from the wind and waves by reefs and barrier islands but are still affected by the ocean tides. Tampa Bay, Charlotte Harbor, and Indian River Lagoon are examples of estuaries found in Florida.

17

What bird—though it's not a Florida native—makes many people think of Florida?

A The flamingo. More than 400 live in Hialeah.

Henry Flagler

Henry Flagler, who had become wealthy as a founder of the Standard Oil Company, moved to St. Augustine in 1885, where he built the Hotel Ponce de León and the Alcazar. He built the Florida East Coast Railway, which traveled the length of the Florida Peninsula and eventually all the way down the Keys to Key West. He also built several more hotels such as the Royal Poinciana Hotel and The Breakers in Palm Beach. His railroad and hotel empire encouraged tourism and trade in Florida.

Fort Clinch

In 1847 construction began on Fort Clinch, located on the northeast tip of Amelia Island, as far north and east as you can get in Florida. The fort, surrounded by a brick wall, was designed to house 550 soldiers and covers an area about 100 yards long by 100 yards wide. The fort was named for General Duncan Lamont Clinch, a general in the Second Seminole War.

Ford, Fruit Trees, and Fort Myers

Henry Ford, the car manufacturer, and his wife, Clara, often visited Thomas Edison's winter estate in Fort Myers. In 1916 they decided to purchase Mangoes, the estate next door to the Edison's home. During their vacations to Mangoes, the Fords planted a garden filled with tropical fruit trees—citrus, papayas, and mangoes!

Fossils

One of the greatest places to hunt for fossils in North America is Florida. Strange and wonderful animals roamed the place we call Florida for over 50 million years. Their remains can be located in lakes, springs, and oceans throughout the state. Fossilized bones and shark teeth can be found along the many riverbanks and beaches. Limestone quarries reveal a wealth of unusual fossils.

Giant sloth fossil

Mangoes

baby flamingo

19

GO

Gopher Tortoise

The ancient-looking gopher tortoise has a dome-shaped shell, eats grasses, and lives in well-drained sandy areas in Florida. It makes its home in an underground burrow, which is also home to many other species such as rattlesnakes, Florida mice, and gopher frogs. A burrow can be as long as 30 feet. Tiny hatchling gopher tortoises number from an average of 5 or 6 per clutch to as many as 25. The gopher tortoise has been identified as a Species of Special Concern in Florida. The population of these reptiles has dwindled because of habitat destruction from man-made development.

Gainesville

The city of Gainesville, named for the Seminole War hero Edmund Gaines, was created in 1854. Gainesville was a citrus capital until freezes ended this agricultural industry for Alachua County. In 1906, the University of Florida opened in Gainesville and began classes with 102 students.

Jean Craighead George

Jean Craighead George is a Newbery Award–winning children's author who writes books about nature. The Missing Gator of Gumbo Limbo and The Talking Earth are two of her books that are set in the wilds of Florida.

Gasparilla Pirate Festival

Every February "pirates" sail into Tampa Bay in hundreds of ships and take over the city in a three-day street party. The festival was named after José Gaspar, a pirate of legend or history—no one knows for sure. Rumor has it that he buried over 20 chests of gold and jewels somewhere in Florida. Along with a parade of pirates, the city of Tampa celebrates Gasparilla Days with an art show, street music, lots of food, and fireworks.

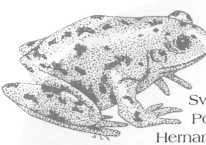

Green Swamp

The Green Swamp, located in Polk, Lake, Sumter, Hernando, and Pasco Counties, is one of the most important ground-water recharge areas in the state of Florida. This vital area is the beginning of several rivers, including the Hillsborough, Withlacoochee, Oklawaha, and Peace Rivers. In addition to providing a potable (drinkable) water supply, the Green Swamp is also habitat to many wildlife species.

John Gorrie

Dr. John Gorrie was a physician from Apalachicola, Florida. In 1851, he invented an ice-making machine to cool the hospital rooms of yellow fever patients. He was granted the first U.S. patent for refrigeration and worked on experiments to make ice. A statue of Dr. Gorrie was placed in the U. S. Capitol to honor this great Floridian whose invention was the model for what we know as air conditioning.

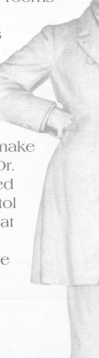

Gulf Islands National Seashore

Gulf Islands National Seashore stretches from Fort Walton Beach in the Florida Panhandle to Gulfport, Mississippi. The park has white sandy beaches, a nineteenth-century fort, nature trails, campsites, and rich coastal marshes.

Horse

In 1935, the first thoroughbred horse farm in Marion County, called Rosemere, was established. Twenty years later, an unknown thoroughbred named Needles won the Kentucky Derby and the Belmont Stakes, putting Marion County on the map for horse breeding. In 1999, Marion County was recognized by the U.S. Department of Agriculture as the Horse Capital of the World. The Ocala area is now home to more than 450 thoroughbred farms with over 50 different horse breeds. Horses come in all sizes in Florida, from the huge draft horse to the miniature horse seen here.

Heron

The great blue heron can be found in Florida, wading in the shallow waters of ponds, rivers, lakes, and marshes. It feeds mainly on fish and frogs but also eats small reptiles, birds, and mammals. This large grayish bird with a yellow bill lives in colonies and lays 3 to 5 greenish-blue eggs.

Ernest Hemingway

One of the most famous American authors is Ernest Miller Hemingway. He wrote the renowned World War I novel *A Farewell to Arms* while living in the Florida Keys. He won the Nobel Prize for Literature in 1954 for his book *The Old Man and the Sea*.

23

Hurricanes

A hurricane is a large, destructive storm measuring several hundred miles across. The winds of a hurricane, which blow in a counterclockwise direction, begin at 74 mph and can be as strong as 200 mph. The center, known as the eye, is approximately 20 miles across and is usually cloudless and has little wind. Hurricane season lasts from June through November in Florida, as it does in the entire Northern Hemisphere. Florida has more major hurricanes than any other state.

Horse Conch

The vibrant pink and orange horse conch was named the state shell in 1969. This marine mollusk can be found off the coastal waters of Florida and can grow as long as 24 inches!

Hialeah Park

Hialeah Park near Miami is home to the famous Hialeah Racecourse, where thoroughbred horses from around the world come to race. The park is in the National Register of Historic Places, and the Audubon Society has designated it a sanctuary for the American flamingo as well. These large, pink wading birds live in the 32-acre infield lake.

Intracoastal Waterway

The Intracoastal Waterway of Florida, an inland water highway for boats, is made up of three connecting sections. The first is the Atlantic Intracoastal Waterway, which extends from Fernandina Beach south to Miami. The second, called the Okeechobee Waterway, extends from Stuart on the east coast, across the Florida peninsula, to Fort Myers on the west coast. The third, the West Coast Intracoastal Waterway, completes the highway, ending in Tarpon Springs.

Immokalee

For many years Immokalee has been a peaceful farming community in Collier County, growing mostly vegetables and citrus. It is now also home to the Seminole Indian Casino, which brings many tourists to this small, southwest Florida town.

Ibis

The white ibis is a wading bird with a curved beak. Ibis roost in large colonies in mangroves along the coasts. Their rich droppings act as fertilizer, increasing the growth of plankton, the main food of marsh life.

Ichetucknee Springs State Park

Tubing down the Ichetucknee River on a sweltering Florida summer day is the activity of choice for many natives and tourists. The 3-hour float takes you past shaded waters and towering cypress trees. Sunning turtles and alligators line the banks of this cold, spring-fed river.

Insects

The warm, humid climate of Florida makes it a perfect home for thousands of species of beneficial and harmful insects. Some helpful insects, such as bees, pollinate flowers, providing fruits and vegetables for humans to enjoy. Fire ants, fleas, mosquitoes, roaches, and termites are just a few of the many insect pests that plague Floridians.

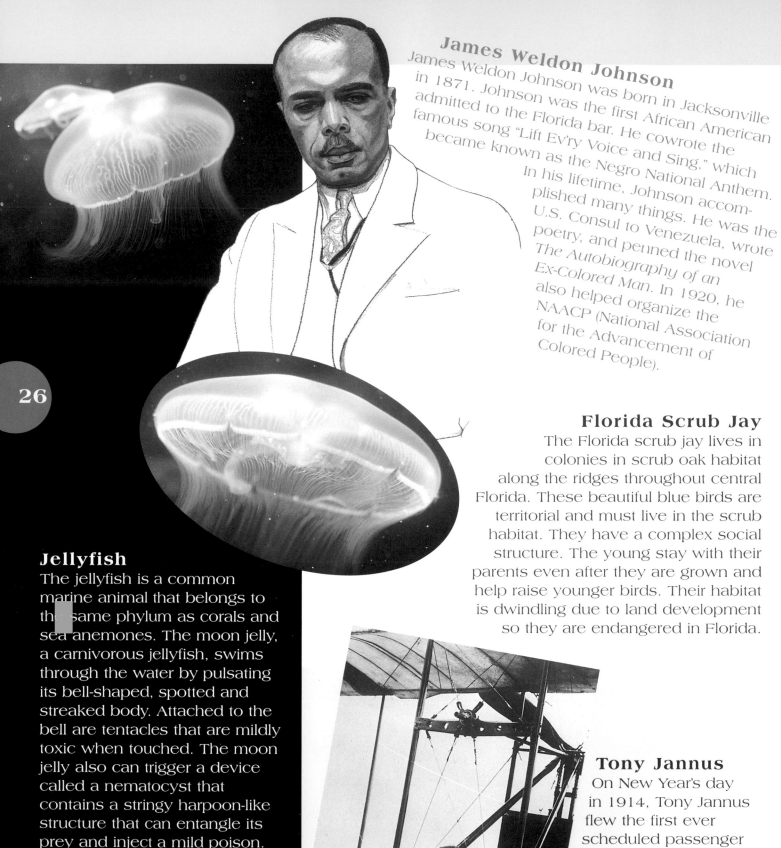

James Weldon Johnson

James Weldon Johnson was born in Jacksonville in 1871. Johnson was the first African American admitted to the Florida bar. He cowrote the famous song "Lift Ev'ry Voice and Sing," which became known as the Negro National Anthem. In his lifetime, Johnson accomplished many things. He was the U.S. Consul to Venezuela, wrote poetry, and penned the novel *The Autobiography of an Ex-Colored Man*. In 1920, he also helped organize the NAACP (National Association for the Advancement of Colored People).

26

Florida Scrub Jay

The Florida scrub jay lives in colonies in scrub oak habitat along the ridges throughout central Florida. These beautiful blue birds are territorial and must live in the scrub habitat. They have a complex social structure. The young stay with their parents even after they are grown and help raise younger birds. Their habitat is dwindling due to land development so they are endangered in Florida.

Jellyfish

The jellyfish is a common marine animal that belongs to the same phylum as corals and sea anemones. The moon jelly, a carnivorous jellyfish, swims through the water by pulsating its bell-shaped, spotted and streaked body. Attached to the bell are tentacles that are mildly toxic when touched. The moon jelly also can trigger a device called a nematocyst that contains a stringy harpoon-like structure that can entangle its prey and inject a mild poison. The Portuguese man-of-war is another kind of jellyfish that can be found in the Gulf Stream off the east coast of Florida. This animal has tentacles that can be 65 feet in length! The sting of this jellyfish can be painful to humans and has sent many people to the hospital for relief.

Tony Jannus

On New Year's day in 1914, Tony Jannus flew the first ever scheduled passenger airline flight. The airplane, a Benoist Model 14, flew from St. Petersburg to Tampa, across Tampa Bay.

"Tony Jannus" Benoist Air Boat

Jai Alai

Jai alai (pronounced *high lie*), the world's fastest ball game, originated in the Basque region of Spain. Jai alai, which means "joyous festival" in Basque, is played against a wall using a *cesta*, a curved wicker basket, and a *pelota*, a small goatskin-covered ball. The speed of the pelota, which is smaller than a baseball and harder than a golf ball, has been clocked at 180 mph. There are more jai alai frontons, or arenas, in Florida than anywhere else in the world.

cesta

Jacksonville

Florida's largest city in area at 841 square miles is located at the mouth of the St. Johns River in northeast Florida. It is a deep-water port of entry. Named after Andrew Jackson, the city was burned to the ground during the Civil War and rebuilt, later becoming the leading industrial city in Florida. Today, Jacksonville is a major transportation and commerce center from which paper products, lumber, automobiles, machinery, and other goods are shipped all over the world.

27

Karst Terrain

Areas in Florida that have karst terrain have many caves, springs, sinkholes, and sinkhole lakes. (*Kars* is a Yugoslavian word that means "stone" and has been used to describe an area in Yugoslavia that boasts this landscape.) Water seeping through an underground limestone layer creates these karst features. Approximately 630 caves have been located in Florida by the Florida Speleological Society, whose members study and explore caves.

Kaolin

Kaolin is a fine white clay, also known as china clay, that does not discolor during firing. During the late 1700s, kaolin was extracted from bluffs at the E. F. Skinner Mill near Pensacola. It was shipped to England to make elegant white pipes and Wedgwood pottery.

Key West and the Florida Keys

Key West

The Florida Keys are a coral-and-limestone island chain that stretches 192 miles from Virginia Key, just south of Miami Beach, to Loggerhead Key in the Dry Tortugas. The city of Key West holds the title of southernmost city in the continental United States. This small coral island, the largest of the Florida Keys, is approximately 4 miles long and 2 miles wide. Tourism and fishing are the main industries on the island. Seven miles off its coast is some of the best coral reef diving in the world. US Route 1 begins in Key West with mile marker zero.

Kennedy Space Center

The John F. Kennedy Space Center is located on Cape Canaveral, a peninsula on the Atlantic Coast of Florida. The visitor center offers an IMAX theater, bus tours, a space museum, and even a rocket garden with actual rockets on display. Several times a year, the space shuttle is launched from the space center. Thousands of visitors line the causeways to watch the liftoff.

32 inches

Key Deer

Key deer are located only in the lower Keys of Florida. Sometimes called toy deer because they grow only as tall as 32 inches, their population numbers between 600 and 800 members. Key deer spend most of their time foraging for food and eat leaves from plants like gumbo limbo trees and red mangroves.

Kingsley Plantation

Zephaniah Kingsley established a cotton plantation on Fort George Island, near Fernandina Beach, Florida, in 1813. He settled there with his wife, Anna, an ex-slave, and their children. The family and 60 slaves produced Sea Island cotton, citrus, sugar cane, and corn. The Kingsley Plantation is now a National Historic Site where visitors can view the main residence, barn, and remains of 23 slave cabins.

Lightning

More people are killed or injured from lightning in Florida than any other place in the nation. Lightning bolts hotter than 25,000 degrees have been known to cause trees to burst into flames when struck. July and August are the peak lightning season. Florida is also the Thunderstorm Capital of the United States. Thunderstorms usually last less than two hours and occur in the afternoon.

Largemouth Bass

In 1975, the largemouth bass was named Florida's State Freshwater Fish. This black bass can grow to 20 pounds and has an exceptionally large mouth and a notched dorsal fin. Females can lay up to 25,000 eggs at a time. Adult bass live in still, plant-filled waters.

Lighthouses

In order to alert seagoing vessels to dangerous reefs and safe harbors, lighthouses were built up and down the coastline of Florida. Gone are the lighthouse keepers of the past, because the lanterns inside lighthouses are now turned on and off by timers and solar cells. Today in Florida 32 lighthouses remain standing. Most are now operated by the U. S. Coast Guard. Some are only daymarks, and a few are now museums.

Q What is the **largest** lake in Florida?

A Lake Okeechobee

30

Lakes

There are over 7,800 lakes in Florida. Over half of them are found on the sandy ridges of central Florida. Formed mostly from ancient sinkholes, these lakes are important to the recharge (refilling) of the Floridan Aquifer, where we get most of our drinking water. Lake Okeechobee, the largest lake in Florida, measures 470,000 acres.

Love Bugs

Love bugs appear in Florida twice a year from April through May and September through October. They are called love bugs because they fly together while they mate. They can form large swarms that fill the air, smashing into cars and creating a sticky mess for travelers.

Jacques LeMoyne

Jacques LeMoyne, a French artist, explored Florida with René de Laudonnière in 1564. LeMoyne documented his journey with writings and drawings of the Timucua Indians he encountered. He also drew this early map, which was used as the main map of the area for over 100 years. Laudonnière and his group established a settlement on the St. Johns River, where they built Fort Caroline. The fort was burned by the Spanish along with LeMoyne's drawings. When he returned to France he redrew them from memory! They were published in a book of engravings by Theodore DeBry, along with LeMoyne's descriptions of Florida.

M

Manatee

The manatee lives in the warm waters of Florida's rivers and springs during the cold winter months. This marine mammal can grow as long as 13 feet and can weigh between 1,200 and 3,500 pounds. To maintain this great weight, the manatee must eat 60 to 100 pounds of aquatic plants daily. Manatees have no natural predators. The greatest danger they face is from the propellers of speeding boats. Over half of all manatee deaths are caused by humans.

Moonstone

To commemorate the lunar landing of U.S. astronauts Buzz Aldrin and Neil Armstrong during the *Apollo 11* mission, the moonstone became the official Florida State Gem in 1970. This iridescent silvery-blue stone is not found in Florida or on the moon but comes from Sri Lanka, a country in Asia!

Mangroves

There are more than 500,000 acres of mangroves in Florida. Mangroves are the habitat for hundreds of species of birds, fish, reptiles, and amphibians. They filter out pollution from the water and protect the shoreline from erosion. Fish and shellfish populations decline when mangroves are destroyed.

What are the **3 kinds** of mangroves found in Florida ?

Red, black, and white mangroves.

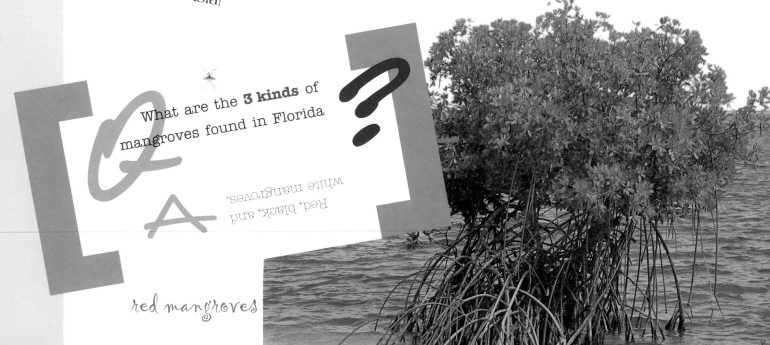

red mangroves

Mosquito

The bite you get from a mosquito is always from a female because the female mosquito needs blood in order for her eggs to form. Mosquitoes lay their eggs in stagnant water found in swamps and ditches, as well as old tires, flowerpots, and gutters. The eggs need to be covered in water in order to hatch.

Miami

The city of Miami is located on the banks of the Miami River, where it empties into Biscayne Bay in southeast Florida. Since Flagler extended his railroad from West Palm Beach to Miami after the freeze of 1895, Miami has become a thriving industrial city. Miami Beach, on the barrier island east of Miami, is famed for its Art Dcco architecture shown here.

Don Pedro Menéndez

Spain sent Don Pedro Menéndez de Avilés to be the new governor of Florida in 1565. After burning the French garrison already there, he founded the colony of St. Augustine, established a mission for the Native Americans, built a fort, and explored the surrounding land.

Missions

Franciscan friars built a chain of missions in Florida. The missions were used to teach the Christian religion to Native Americans. The friars also taught farming, cattle raising, and reading. In return, the Native Americans were expected to protect the Spanish from French and English soldiers as well as other Indian tribes.

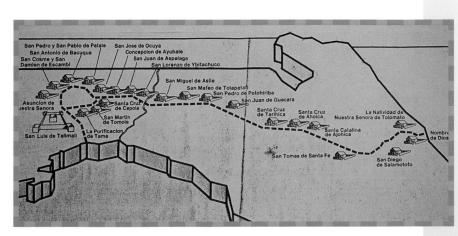

NASA

The National Aeronautics and Space Administration (NASA) is a government agency created in 1958 in response to the Soviet Union's launch of *Sputnik*, the first artificial satellite. The agency was given the job to research and develop space exploration. NASA has launched satellites for many purposes, such as enhancing global communications and collecting information on weather. The Apollo Program, which put a man on the moon, the Space Shuttle Program, and the International Space Station are examples of NASA's accomplishments.

Nuestra Señora de Atocha

During a hurricane on September 5, 1622, the Spanish Royal Guard galleon, the *Nuestra Señora de Atocha*, sank in the Gulf of Mexico off the Florida Keys. For hundreds of years, treasure hunters have searched for the *Atocha*, which carried silver bars, chests of silver coins, jewels, and gold. Mel Fisher and his family spent 16 years diving off the coast, looking for the lost treasure ship. On July 20, 1985, Fisher received a radio message from his son Kane that the multimillion dollar treasure had been located!

Ninety-Mile Prairie

Between the Kissimmee River and Charlotte Harbor exists a large expanse of palmetto prairie. In the late 1800s, before fences were erected across the land, Florida cowboys would drive cattle across the Ninety-Mile Prairie to Punta Rassa, a deep-water shipping point just north of Ft. Myers. Here, the cowboys would sell their herd for a profit, and the cows would be shipped to other markets. Florida remained a wild frontier with a thriving cattle industry long after the Wild West was tamed.

Battle of Natural Bridge

Located in Wakulla County on the St. Marks River, Natural Bridge is a place where the river runs underground for a few feet and then re-emerges, forming a natural bridge. During the last months of the Civil War, the Union army marched to attack the fort at St. Marks. The Confederate soldiers felt that Tallahassee was in danger. On March 6, 1865, the Battle of Natural Bridge began. A small group of Confederate troops successfully stopped the Union soldiers from crossing Natural Bridge and taking Tallahassee. Tallahassee remained the only Southern capital east of the Mississippi River to remain in Southern control throughout the Civil War.

Natural Bridge

National Museum of Naval Aviation

At Pensacola Naval Air Station, the museum collects, preserves, and displays memorabilia that show the development and growth of United States naval aviation. There are more than 130 aircraft on display that span the history of naval aviation, from 1911 to the present time.

ghost orchid

Orchids
Of the 157 species of orchids growing in North America, about 110 grow in Florida. Orchids can be found in the wild attached to tree limbs and even growing on rocks. The Fakahatchee Strand is home to the elusive and sought-after ghost orchid.

Osprey
These long-winged hawks that nest near water in tall trees such as cypress or pines also build their large, bulky nests in man-made structures like telephone poles and antennas. They fly high over the water, searching for prey. When the osprey spots a fish, it swoops down and plunges feet-first into the water, gripping the fish with its spiked talons.

Overseas Highway
The Overseas Highway was built over the same route as Henry Flagler's Florida East Coast Railway, which was partially destroyed by a hurricane in 1935. Located in the Florida Keys, this highway travels south from the mainland to Key West and is the longest overseas road in the world. It contains 42 bridges, including the famous Seven-mile Bridge.

Seven-mile Bridge

36

Ocala National Forest

The Ocala National Forest, located in central Florida, is the oldest national forest east of the Mississippi River. It covers over 384,000 acres of wilderness. Juniper Springs and Alexander Springs are just two of the many recreation areas in the forest that provide swimming, camping, and canoeing opportunities for visitors. Some of the best bass fishing can be found in the many lakes and ponds in the Ocala National Forest.

"Old Folks at Home"

Stephen Foster wrote the song "Old Folks at Home," which begins "Way down upon the Swanee (Suwannee) River," in 1851. It became the official Florida State Song in 1935. "I Dream of Jeannie with the Light Brown Hair" is also among the 200 songs that Foster wrote. A memorial center was built in his honor in White Springs.

Henry Plant

Henry B. Plant was a wealthy businessman from Connecticut who started the railroad boom in Florida. Plant built rails from Jacksonville, along the St. Johns River to Sanford, then on to Tampa. He built the Tampa Bay Hotel on the Hillsboro River to attract wealthy tourists to the area. His railroad also brought business, like cigar manufacturing, to Tampa.

brown pelican

Pelican

There are two kinds of pelicans found in Florida. The smaller, brown pelican is a year-round resident of Florida, while the larger, white pelican spends most of the year in the Northern states and winters in Florida Bay.

The Tampa Bay Hotel, now the University of Tampa

Parasailing

A sport that has gained popularity along the beaches of Florida is parasailing. A brave participant is strapped into a body harness and pulled along behind a boat. The parasail lifts the person high into the air, where the parasailor can maneuver by pulling on lines.

Pine Tree

Pine forests are abundant throughout Florida. The longleaf pine, also known as yellow pine, is used for building and construction. The sap is used for making tar, pitch, and turpentine. The longleaf pine ecosystem once covered 90 million acres in the United States. Now only 3 million acres remain. This endangered ecosystem has been the target of restoration projects in Florida and other Southern states.

Ponce de León

Juan Ponce de León landed on the coast of Florida near present-day St. Augustine in April 1513. He was searching for the legendary Fountain of Youth. Ponce de León thought he had landed on an island and did not know he was actually on the mainland of North America. He named the land "*La Florida*" because of its beautiful flowers and lush vegetation. It was also Easter and the Spanish word for this holiday is *Pascua Florida.*

Panther

This 6-foot-long, pale brown cat has been on the endangered species list since 1967. It has been illegal to hunt and kill panthers since 1958. The Latin name for the Florida panther is *Felis concolor coryi.* In 1982, the students of Florida voted to make the panther the Florida State Animal.

Quilts

Colonial women in America created beautiful bed covers called quilts using scraps of fabric sewn together in bold designs. They used their fine needle-working skills to produce many colorful, warm, and useful quilts. The Museum of Florida History, located in Tallahassee, houses the Florida Quilt Collection, which includes fifty examples of quilts made in Florida from the 1830s to the present time.

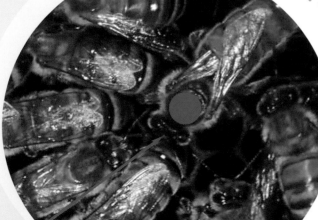

Queen

(marked with red dot)

Queen Bee

The first queen bee to emerge from the egg destroys all the other hatching queens and becomes the queen bee of the hive. She lives for about five years, mating with drones and laying eggs. Honey bees make approximately 25,000 round trips from the flower to the hive to make one pound of honey. Tupelo honey is produced from tupelo gum trees that grow along the banks of the Apalachicola, Choctawhatchee, and Ochlockonee Rivers in northwest Florida.

Peggy Ann Quince

Peggy Ann Quince is the first African-American woman appointed to the Florida Supreme Court. She was appointed by Governor Lawton Chiles and Governor-elect Jeb Bush in 1998. Quince had served as an appellate judge, private practitioner, and assistant attorney general.

Quincy

The county seat of Gadsen County, Quincy is located 20 miles west of Tallahassee. The population of Quincy is approximately 7,400. Before the Civil War, money came from cotton, then tobacco—after that came Coca-Cola! A local banker urged his friends to buy stock in the drink, and since the stock only cost two cents a share in the 1920s, an original investment of $1,000 was worth $2.5 million by 1994. For a while Quincy, known as "the Coca-Cola town," was the richest small town in the U.S.

Quail

The bobwhite quail is a small game bird that is found in a variety of habitats, ranging from open fields and woodlands to parks. Quail spend their lives traveling in coveys, or small groups, of 5 to 30 birds, which give protection from predators and provide warmth in the winter months. Quail live on the ground, where they eat, sleep, and build their nests, rising suddenly into the air as a group when disturbed by predators.

Marjorie Kinnan Rawlings

Marjorie Kinnan Rawlings received a Pulitzer Prize in Literature for *The Yearling*, the story of a boy and his fawn set in the backwoods of Florida. Rawlings bought 68 acres in a small town near Gainesville called Cross Creek in 1928. A former newspaper reporter, she made a living growing citrus and writing novels. Her home in Cross Creek is now a historic state park.

Riverboat

From the 1830s to the 1880s, riverboats were the most important method of transportation in Florida. The St. Johns River was the major waterway for these steamboats, linking Jacksonville to other small Southern towns along the river and its tributaries. The riverboat carried tourists and manufactured goods to towns along the way. Farmers also found the riverboat a quick and easy method to get their produce to market. Once the cheaper and faster railroads were built, the use of riverboats declined.

Roseate Spoonbill

This unusual bird has brilliant pink and white plumage with a flattened, spoon-shaped bill. The roseate spoonbill can be found feeding on shrimp and fish in the shallows of the Gulf of Mexico and Florida Bay. At the turn of the century, roseate spoonbills were killed by plume hunters, who sold their colorful feathers for hat decorations.

Resurrection Fern

During periods of dry weather in Florida, if you look high into a huge live oak tree, you will see a dead-looking plant with curled-up leaves attached to the top sides of the branches. When it rains, the resurrection fern unfurls its leaves, turns green, and springs back to life. The word *resurrect* means to come back to life!

John Ringling

John Ringling purchased the Barnum and Bailey Circus in London in 1907. He traveled with the circus in Europe, then brought the circus to Sarasota in the summer of 1929. While summering in Sarasota, he built an Italian Renaissance home and an art museum to house his personal art collection. When he died, he left his home, museum, and art collection to the State of Florida. Control of the circus was given to his nephew, John Ringling North.

6-inches!

S

44

What **plant** attaches to tree branches and is a member of the pineapple family?

A. Spanish moss.

Saber-toothed Cat

Fossils of saber-toothed cats have been found in central Florida. These carnivores lived approximately 35,000 years ago during the Ice Age. They could run very fast and had 6-inch-long, saber-shaped teeth, which they used to puncture the hide of their prey. The saber-toothed cat became extinct when the climate changed at the end of the Ice Age.

Sunshine Skyway Bridge

In 1980, a freighter hit the Sunshine Skyway Bridge in Tampa Bay, causing the bridge to collapse. A new bridge, which took five years to build, was completed in May 1987 at a cost of $244 million. Designed by engineer Jean Muller, the new Sunshine Skyway Bridge won a 1988 Presidential Award for Design Excellence. This bridge is the world's longest cable-stayed concrete bridge and the most colorful. The cables are painted a vivid yellow!

cables →

Seminole Indians

In 1830, the Indian Relocation Act was passed, requiring all Florida Indians to move to reservations in Oklahoma. A small band of Seminoles eluded capture and hid in the Everglades. Today, the more than 2,000 descendants of those Indians live on six reservations throughout the state and have become financially independent. The Florida Seminoles call themselves the "unconquered people." Seminole Indian dolls are just a small part of the rich cultural history of the Seminole tribe. Colorful dolls have become highly collectible.

Sponge

Sponges harvested from the ocean are the skeletons of marine animals that were once alive. In the 1930s, the sponge capital of the world was Tarpon Springs. The sponge industry brought millions of dollars to Florida's economy. Then, in the 1940s, the sponge beds were destroyed by bacteria. Healthy sponge beds were discovered in the 1980s, and the industry was revived. Today, once again, Tarpon Springs is a leader in the world sponge market.

State Seal

The Florida State Seal was revised in 1985 to correct some errors in the original seal. The Western Plains Indian was changed to a Seminole Indian woman, the cocoa palm was changed to the sabal palm, and the steamboat was drawn more accurately. The original seal was designed in 1868.

original seal

new seal

Tourists

What kid wouldn't want to go to *Florida* on vacation? Beaches, theme parks, museums, deep-sea fishing, the Kennedy Space Center, and many other attractions make tourism the largest industry in the state. Over 40 million snowbirds spend $35 billion when they visit Florida each year.

Tamiami Trail

The building of the Tamiami Trail, which connected the cities of Tampa and Miami through the Everglades, was completed in 1928. Rocks had to be blasted out of the ground with dynamite and then piled up to make the roadbed. A water-filled canal formed where the rocks had been removed. Recently, a 55-mile stretch of the Tamiami Trail, from Collier-Seminole State Park to the Dade County line, was declared a Florida Scenic Highway.

Louis Comfort Tiffany

The Morse Museum in Winter Park has an extensive collection of glass masterpieces by the famous artist Lewis Comfort Tiffany. The highly prized Tiffany lamps are among the beautiful treasures to be found in this collection. Tiffany stained glass windows (like the one shown) can also be seen at the old Ponce de Leon Hotel, now part of Flagler College, in St.Augustine.

Tampa

Tampa is the third largest city in the state of Florida. Home to the Buccaneers and the Devil Rays, Tampa is also the industrial and trading center of the west coast of Florida. The University of South Florida and the University of Tampa are located in Tampa.

Tallahassee

When Florida became a territory, it needed a centrally located capital city. Tallahassee, a small Indian village located between St. Augustine and Pensacola, was chosen as the capital. Three log cabins were built and served as the first capitol buildings. Today, Tallahassee is the seat of Leon County and is home to Florida State University and Florida Agriculture and Mechanical University.

Tabby

Tabby construction was used in St. Augustine beginning in the late 1600s. Tabby is a mixture of lime, sand, and oyster shells that forms a cement. The wet tabby was poured into a wooden form to create walls, floors, and even roof slabs. Most remaining tabby construction can be found along the southern coast of the United States. The Castillo de San Marcos in St. Augustine was built using tabby and coquina.

tabby

Timucua Indians

The Timucua Indians were a highly civilized culture living in the central and northeast parts of Florida when the first European explorers arrived. The people of the tribe had tattoos and wore shell and bead ornaments. They fastened their hair with bone pins. The Timucuans were farmers as well as hunters and fishermen. They lived in round huts with palm leaves for roofs. Each village was surrounded by walls made of poles.

Umatilla Black Bear Festival

Umatilla, the "Gateway to the Ocala National Forest," is home to the annual Black Bear Festival. Held each fall, the festival celebrates the black bear with educational exhibits that provide information on protecting this species. Music, food, crafts, and presentations by Florida authors are just some of the activities during this weekend extravaganza.

Union Jack

Five flags have flown over the state of Florida: English, French, Spanish, Confederate, and American. The Union Jack is the name of the English flag that flew over Florida from 1763 to 1783. In 1763, Spain gave Florida to England in exchange for Havana, Cuba, which had been captured by the English. St. Augustine was named the capital of England's new territory. The English gave Florida back to Spain in 1783 in exchange for the Bahama Islands after England lost the Revolutionary War.

The Union Jack flew over Florida from 1763 to 1783.

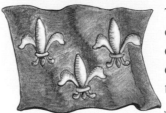

This flag briefly flew over a French colony, commanded by René de Laudonnière, near the mouth of the St. Johns River in 1564.

Union is the tiny red part!

Union County

In 1929, Union County became the 61st county in Florida. Union County is the smallest Florida county in area: only 240 square miles. Its name was derived from the word "unity" since its founders hoped the county would bring together several small communities in the area.

State Universities

Florida has 10 state universities, which grant over 35,000 baccalaureate degrees each year. These universities train businesspeople, scientists, engineers, lawyers, teachers, doctors, and many other professionals. Research and development of new technologies is an important part of the state university system.

The Spanish flag flew off and on over Florida for over 300 years; from 1513, when Ponce de León claimed Florida for Spain; after Pedro Menéndez de Avilés founded St. Augustine in 1565; and again after the British period until 1821.

The Confederate Stars and Bars flew over Florida from 1861 until 1865.

Florida became a territory of the United States of America in 1821 and a state in 1845. This flag shows 27 stars since Florida was the 27th state to be admitted to the Union.

Union Blockade

A week after the Civil War began at Fort Sumter on April 12, 1861, President Abraham Lincoln declared a blockade of all ports in the South. Florida, the third state to secede from the Union, was important to the Confederacy for shipping cattle north to feed the army. The Union navy placed ships along the coast of Florida to prevent beef, salt, and other goods from reaching the Confederate soldiers. While trying to help the Confederate cause, many ships were captured running the blockade.

VIEW OF NEW FERNANDINA AND CEDAR KEYS RAILWAY, OCCUPIED BY THE NATIONAL NAVAL AND LAND FORCES UNDER COMMODORE DUPONT AND GE

Volusia County

Volusia County is home to cities such as Daytona Beach and New Smyrna Beach. Tourism is the number one industry in Volusia County. Visitors flock to the hard-sand beaches on the Atlantic coast. On the banks of the St. Johns River, which runs through Volusia County, you can find shell middens (mounds) left by ancient Native Americans. Remains of old sugar and indigo plantations dot the countryside. Blue dye made from the indigo plant is used for denim blue jeans.

indigo spire

blue jeans

Vegetables

Florida is the second leading vegetable producer in the United States, providing the nation with 20 percent of all the vegetables sold. Approximately $1.7 billion worth of vegetables are produced in Florida each year.

Vulture

There are two kinds of vultures found in Florida: the turkey vulture and the black vulture. Sometimes called buzzards, both kinds of vultures are scavengers, feeding on carrion (dead animals), garbage, and decaying vegetation. Black vultures are more aggressive and smaller than turkey vultures. Unlike turkey vultures, they cannot locate carrion by smell but must use their keen eyesight. Vultures roost and nest in communities.

Valencia Oranges

Approximately half of the oranges planted and harvested in Florida are Valencia oranges. Because Valencia oranges are difficult to section and have seeds, they are used most often for making juice and juice concentrate. The Valencia is the most widely planted orange in the world.

Venice

The city of Venice, in Sarasota County, is known as the Sharks' Tooth Capital of the World because so many fossilized sharks' teeth wash up on its beaches. White-sand beaches, the warm waters of the Gulf of Mexico, and temperatures that rarely dip below 70 degrees make Venice a beautiful recreation and resort area. Every summer, visitors and residents head to the water-front to enjoy the Sharks' Tooth and Seafood Festival.

Vizcaya

An Italian Renaissance villa built in 1916 in Miami was owned by millionaire industrialist James Deering. Vizcaya was built as a winter home, and he spent only nine winters there. The rooms were designed as if many generations had lived there. The 34 rooms are filled with furniture from the fifteenth through the nineteenth centuries. Vizcaya's formal gardens fill ten acres that show Italian and French gardens along with tropical foliage typical of Florida. Vizcaya has been designated a National Historic Landmark.

James Deering

W

Watermelons

Over 35,000 acres of watermelons are planted and harvested yearly in Florida from December to April. Watermelons bring over $60 million into the Florida economy each year.

William Charles Wells

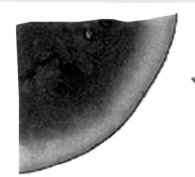

Weedon Island

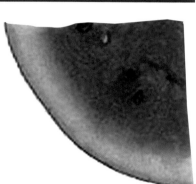

The pre-Columbian Native Americans of the Weedon Island culture lived in the northern half of Florida from 600 A.D. to 1400 A.D. During this period, these natives moved inland to farm in more fertile, upland soils. The people of the Weedon Island culture were known for their intricate pottery designs and ceramic vessels shaped like animals.

The first newspaper in Florida, the *East Florida Gazette*, was published by William Charles Wells. Wells was a loyal Englishman who used his newspaper to attack the Americans during the Revolution. When the Spanish were given control of Florida in 1783, Wells closed the paper and returned to England.

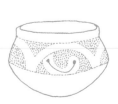

Walt Disney World

Built on land that was once swampland, Walt Disney World is a world-famous resort that boasts several theme parks, hotels, and shopping areas. Located in central Florida near the city of Orlando, it covers approximately 47 square miles. Millions of guests travel from all over the world each year to visit Walt Disney World. Walt Disney sold his first drawing (to a neighbor) when he was only seven years old! He later created the cartoon characters Mickey Mouse and Donald Duck. Disney opened Disneyland in California in 1955. Florida's Walt Disney World opened in 1971.

© Disney Enterprises. Used by permission.

53

Wood Stork

The wood stork nests, feeds, and roosts in colonies in the Everglades and some parts of south Florida. This bird requires a cycle of wet and dry seasons in order to thrive and reproduce. The wood stork, which is the only stork found in the United States, locates its food by swinging its bill back and forth in shallow water. When its bill touches a small fish, it snaps shut faster than the blink of an eye! During a dry season, the fish are concentrated in shallow pools, allowing wood storks enough available food for the breeding season. The population of wood storks has declined sharply and the birds have been on the federal Endangered Species list since 1984.

Worm Grunting

Each spring in the Apalachicola National Forest, near the small town of Sopchoppy, worm baiters can be found collecting worms to sell. Worm baiters use a stake, called a stob, which they pound into the ground. They then rub a long metal bar, called an iron, along the top of the stob. This creates a creaky sound that c-r-e-a-k causes the worms to rise out of the ground. The worms are collected and sold for $25 – 28 per bucket.

stob

c-r-e-a-k

...bait?

X Marks the Spot

Treasure hunting in the waters off the coast of Florida has become a thriving pastime for adventurers like Mel Fisher, who discovered the multi-million-dollar treasure from the wreck of the Spanish ship *Atocha*. Combine the Spanish treasure galleons of the 16th and 17th centuries with Florida hurricanes, throw in a few dangerous reefs, and you have all the makings of a 21st-century treasure hunt!

Ximenez-Fatio House

The two-story coquina block house and store was built in 1798 in St. Augustine by Andres Ximenez, a Spanish merchant. A general store occupied the ground floor and the living quarters were upstairs. There is a separate kitchen building that has the original baking oven made of brick. Miss Louisa Fatio bought the property in 1855 and made it into a fashionable inn that could accommodate 24 guests. It is now owned by the Colonial Dames of America in the State of Florida.

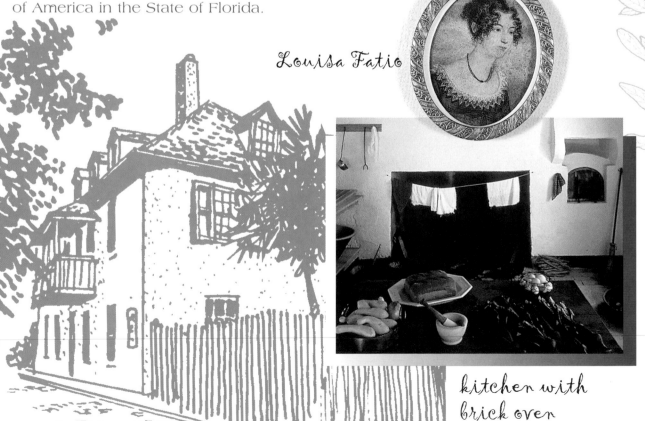

Louisa Fatio

kitchen with brick oven

Xeriscaping

Xeriscaping is a method of landscaping often used in Florida to preserve water. Taking into account drought tolerance as well as light, shade, and soil requirements is important when choosing plants for a Xeriscape plan. Using native plant species helps to reduce water consumption. It is possible to lower water usage from 25 – 75% when homeowners use this method of landscaping.

Xeric Oak Scrub

The xeric oak scrub habitat was formed millions of years ago when ocean water levels were high, forming giant sandy ridges in the middle of the state. The sand is so deep that water percolates quickly through the soil. The Lake Wales Ridge National Wildlife Refuge is home to many endangered species that can live only in this habitat.

LoXahatchee National Wildlife Refuge

The Loxahatchee National Wildlife Refuge is located west of Boynton Beach in Palm Beach County. Because of development and farming, this refuge is the largest remaining natural area of the northern Everglades. Loxahatchee is a Seminole word that means "river of turtles." The Loxahatchee National Wildlife Refuge is known for its excellent bird watching.

Y

Ybor City and Vicente Martinez-Ybor

Ybor City was founded in 1886 when Vicente Martinez-Ybor moved his cigar factory from Key West to Tampa to take advantage of the railroad, the port, and the naturally warm, humid climate. Many immigrants from Cuba, Spain, and Italy came to Ybor City to work in the cigar factories. Ybor City became the "cigar capital of the world," producing over 250 million cigars a year. A combination of the Depression, the popularity of cigarettes, and the introduction of machines to cigar-making ended the successful industry in Tampa. Ybor City is one of three National Historic Landmark Districts in Florida.

Yellow-crowned Night Heron

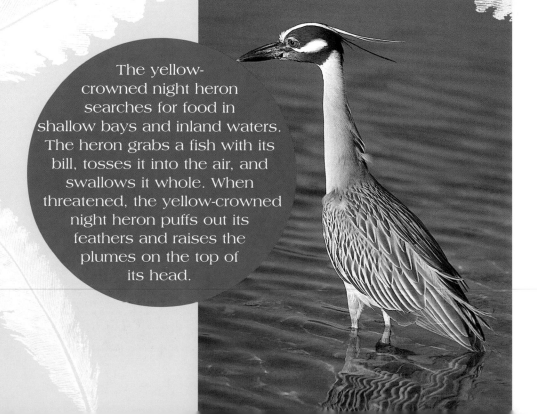

The yellow-crowned night heron searches for food in shallow bays and inland waters. The heron grabs a fish with its bill, tosses it into the air, and swallows it whole. When threatened, the yellow-crowned night heron puffs out its feathers and raises the plumes on the top of its head.

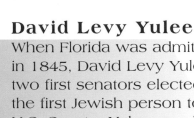

David Levy Yulee

When Florida was admitted to the Union in 1845, David Levy Yulee was one of two first senators elected. He was also the first Jewish person to serve in the U.S. Senate. Yulee was born in the West Indies in 1810 and came to the United States nine years later to attend school. He became a lawyer in 1832 and practiced in St. Augustine. In 1845, he changed his name from David Yulee Levy. The town of Yulee in north Florida is named after him.

Fountain of Youth

Juan Ponce de León led an expedition to find the Fountain of Youth in 1513. He was searching for an island called Bimini but instead landed on the coast of Florida near St. Augustine. Today, tourists drink from a spring in St. Augustine that Ponce de León thought was the fabled Fountain of Youth.

Fountain of Youth

Yankeetown

Yankeetown is located at the southern edge of Levy County on the banks of the Withlacoochee River, the Gulf of Mexico to its west. Agriculture and timber are the main industries of the area. The Izaak Walton Lodge is a landmark in Yankeetown.

Izaak Walton Lodge

Zora Neale Hurston

Zora Neale Hurston was born in 1891 in Eatonville, Florida, the first incorporated all-black town in America. She was educated at Howard University, Barnard College, and Columbia University. She became an author and anthropologist, studying the African-American culture of the South. Hurston influenced the writers of the Harlem Renaissance and, later, authors such as Alice Walker and Toni Morrison. Her most famous book is *Their Eyes Were Watching God*.

antique water bottles

Zephyrhills

In 1886, the town of Abbott was established in Pasco County. The name was changed to Abbott Station when the railroad built a depot for transporting lumber and naval stores such as turpentine and pitch. In 1914, Abbott Station changed its name to Zephyrhills because of its rolling hills and soft breezes. Zephyrhills is known for its cattle ranches, citrus groves, and pure water. In fact, "City of Pure Water" is the nickname of Zephyrhills.

Corn Man

Zellwood Sweet Corn Festival

Each May, the town of Zellwood, just outside of Orlando, celebrates the harvest of sweet corn with a weekend festival. The Zellwood Sweet Corn Festival offers food, amusement rides, music, arts and crafts, and, of course, all the sweet corn you can eat!

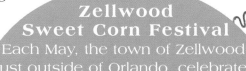

Q What is the name of the state **butterfly**?

A The zebra longwing

Zorayda Castle

Zorayda Castle was built in St. Augustine in 1883 by Franklin Smith. It is a replica of the Alhambra, a twelfth-century Moorish castle in Granada, Spain. The castle has many windows of different sizes so spirits can easily leave but not find their way back in. Zorayda Castle, which contains many antiques and artifacts, is open to the public.

Zoos

There are many zoos and animal attractions in Florida. Many of them have a section on animals native to Florida. The Brevard Zoo has a "paws-on" interactive learning area for children. The Jacksonville Zoo offers a walking safari through the zoo, which contains over 900 animals! Florida also has several wildlife refuges and animal farms that provide a safe haven for hurt or sick animals.

IMAGE CREDITS

Photo research and acquisitions: Alba F. Aragón, Sarah Cussen.

All illustrations by Carol Tornatore unless otherwise noted.

All images shown by permission. Their use does not suggest or imply any endorsement or sponsorship of/by any of the individuals, institutions, or corporations represented herein. Inquiries about image permissions and reproductions must be submitted to the original copyright owner as designated on the credits page.

Adderley, Cannonball: Florida State Archives.
Alligator: Courtesy Everglades Day Safari, www.ecosafari.com.
Apalachicola: Cotton photo by U.S. Department of Agriculture, Agricultural Research Service.
Aquifer: Illustration by Jean Barnes, from *The Florida Water Story* by Peggy Lantz and Wendy Hale © 1988. Published by Pineapple Press, Inc.
Audubon House: Illustration by H. Patrick Reed and Nan E. Wilson, from *Historic Homes of Florida* by Laura Stewart and Susanne Hupp © 1995. Published by Pineapple Press, Inc.
Beaches: VISIT FLORIDA.
Bethune, Mary McLeod: Florida State Archives.
Billy Bowlegs: The Museum of Florida History.
Bok Tower: Courtesy Bok Tower Gardens.
Busch Gardens: © 2002 Busch Entertainment Corporation. All rights reserved.
Castillo de San Marcos: U.S. Department of Interior, National Park Service.
Coreopsis: Florida State Archives.
Cross and Sword: Florida State Archives.
Cross-Florida Barge Canal: Florida State Archives.
Cypress Gardens: © 2002 Florida Cypress Gardens, Inc. All rights reserved.
Cypress Tree: Illustration by Julia Damon Hanway, from *Young Naturalist's Guide to Florida* by Peggy S. Lantz and Wendy A. Hale © 1994. Published by Pineapple Press, Inc.
Daytona Speedway: Race car photo courtesy Carla and Billy Green Photography, Bradenton, Florida.
De Soto, Hernando: Florida State Archives.
Diver: U.S. Department of Commerce, National Oceanic and Atmospheric Administration.
Douglas, Marjory Stoneman: Florida State Archives.

Dry Tortugas: U.S. Department of Interior, National Park Service.
Eagle: Photo by Alan and Sandy Carey/Getty Images.
Eglin Air Force Base: Airplane photo courtesy The National Museum of Naval Aviation.
Egret: Cattle egret photo by Jerry L. Gingerich, from *Common Coastal Birds of Florida and the Caribbean* by David Nellis © 2001. Published by Pineapple Press, Inc.
Estefan, Gloria: Courtesy Estefan Enterprises.
Estuaries: Illustration © 1995 Frank Lohan, from *Florida in Poetry* by Jane A. Jones and Maurice O'Sullivan ©1995. Published by Pineapple Press, Inc.
Everglades: VISIT FLORIDA.
Flagler, Henry: Florida State Archives.
Flamingo: ©2002 Busch Entertainment Corporation. All rights reserved.
Ford Winter Home: Mango photo by June Cussen. Home illustration by H. Patrick Reed and Nan E. Wilson, from *Historic Homes of Florida* by Laura Stewart and Susanne Hupp © 1995. Published by Pineapple Press, Inc.
Fort Clinch: Eric Dusenbery.
Fossils: Courtesy The Museum of Arts and Sciences in Daytona Beach, Florida.
Gainesville: UF clock tower photo by Kevin McCarthy.
Gasparilla Pirate Festival: Courtesy of the Tampa Bay Convention and Visitors Bureau.
George, Jean C: *The Talking Earth* cover art copyright © 1987 by Kam Mak; cover copyright © 1987 by HarperCollins Publishers. Used by permission of HarperCollins Publishers. *The Missing Gator of Gumbo Limbo: An Ecological Mystery* cover art used by permission of HarperCollins Publishers.
Gopher Tortoise: David Nellis.
Gorrie, John: Florida State Archives.
Green Swamp: Frog illustration by Frank Lohan.
Hemingway, Ernest: Florida State Archives.
Heron: VISIT FLORIDA.
Hialeah Park: Florida State Archives.
Horse: Melanie Bowles.
Horse Conch: © The Bailey-Matthews Shell Museum, Sanibel Island, Florida.
Hurricanes: NASA. Image produced by Hal Pierce, Laboratory for Atmospheres, NASA Goddard Space Flight Center.
Ibis: Courtesy Scarlet Colley, www.fin2feather.com.

Ichetucknee Springs State Park: VISIT FLORIDA.

Immokalee: Sign portraying Seminole Indian Jack Tigertail, Florida State Archives.

Insects: Bee photo, United States Department of Agriculture, Agricultural Research Service.

Intracoastal Waterway: Courtesy Florida Inland Navigation District.

Jacksonville: Courtesy City of Jacksonville.

Jai-Alai: Courtesy Dania Jai-Alai, Dania Beach, Florida.

Jannus, Tony: Florida State Archives.

Jay (Florida scrub jay): Courtesy Paula Benshoff, Myakka River State Park.

Jellyfish: Robert M. Myers, courtesy Mote Marine Laboratory.

Johnson, James Weldon: Florida State Archives.

Karst Terrain: VISIT FLORIDA.

Kaolin: Pottery photos by June Cussen

Kennedy Space Center: Space center photo, VISIT FLORIDA. Astronauts photo, Florida State Archives.

Kingsley Plantation: Florida State Archives.

Lakes: NASA.

Largemouth Bass: Illustration by Joel Bewley.

Le Moyne, Jacques: Illustration by Theodore de Bry after Jacques Le Moyne, *Floridae Americae*, 1564-65. Courtesy Birmingham Public Library. From *Art in Florida* by Maybelle Mann © 1999. Published by Pineapple Press, Inc.

Lighthouses: VISIT FLORIDA.

Lightning: U.S. Department of Commerce, National Oceanic and Atmospheric Administration.

Manatee: www.clipart.com

Mangroves: David Nellis.

Menendez, Pedro: Florida State Archives.

Miami: © Bruce Hunt Images.

Missions: Florida State Archives.

Moonstone: Courtesy www.mineralminers.com. Used by permission.

NASA: Shuttle launch photo, VISIT FLORIDA. Man on the moon photo, NASA.

National Museum of Naval Aviation: Courtesy National Museum of Naval Aviation.

Natural Bridge: Florida State Archives.

Ninety-Mile Prairie: Painting by Regina Stahl Briskey, cover art of *Ninety Mile Prairie* by Lee Gramling © 2002. Published by Pineapple Press, Inc.

Nuestra Señora de Atocha: Painting by William Trotter, cover art of *Thirty Florida Shipwrecks* by Kevin McCarthy © 1992. Published by Pineapple Press, Inc.

Ocala National Forest: VISIT FLORIDA.

"Old Folks at Home": Florida State Archives.

Orchids: Ghost orchid photo, © Jeff Ripley. Pink orchids photo, Carol Tornatore.

Osprey: Illustration by Molly Eckler Brown.

Overseas Highway: VISIT FLORIDA.

Panther: VISIT FLORIDA.

Parasailing: VISIT FLORIDA.

Pelican: Photo by David Nellis, from *Common Coastal Birds of Florida and the Caribbean* by David Nellis © 2001. Published by Pineapple Press, Inc.

Pine Tree: Gil Nelson.

Plant, Henry: Courtesy The University of Tampa.

Ponce de León, Juan: Hibiscus flowers photo by June Cussen.

Queen Bee: United States Department of Agriculture, Agricultural Research Service.

Quince, Peggy Ann: Florida State Archives.

Quincy: Coca-Cola historic photos, Florida State Archives.

Quilts: The Museum of Florida History.

Rawlings, Marjorie Kinnan: Courtesy Marjorie Kinnan Rawlings Historic State Park.

Ringling, John: Courtesy The John and Mable Ringling Museum of Art.

Riverboat: Florida State Archives.

Roseate Spoonbill: Illustration by Karl Karalus, cover art of *Florida's Birds* by Herbert W. Kale, II, and David S. Maehr © 1990. Published by Pineapple Press, Inc.

Saber-toothed Cat: Photo by Judy Cutchins, from *Ice Age Giants of the South* by Judy Cutchins and Ginny Johnston © 2000. Published by Pineapple Press, Inc.

Seminoles: Craft doll photo courtesy Collection of the St. Petersburg Museum of History. From *Art in Florida* by Maybelle Mann © 1999. Published by Pineapple Press, Inc.

Sponge Industry: Courtesy Tarpon Springs Chamber of Commerce.

State Seal: Original and present-day seals, Florida State Archives.

Sunshine Skyway: David Nellis.

Tabby: Photo ©1995 by Ken Barrett, Jr. From *The Houses of St. Augustine* by David Nolan ©1995. Published by Pineapple Press, Inc.

Tallahassee: VISIT FLORIDA.

Tamiami Trail: Florida State Archives.

Tiffany, Louis Comfort: Bacchus-style stained-glass window by Louis Comfort Tiffany. Photograph by Ken Barrett Jr. courtesy of Flagler College, St. Augustine, Florida. From *Art in Florida* by Maybelle Mann © 1999. Published by Pineapple Press, Inc.

Timucua Indians: Theodore de Bry after Jacques Le Moyne. *The King and Queen Take a Walk*, 1564. Courtesy Birmingham Public Library. From *Art in Florida* by Maybelle Mann © 1999. Published by Pineapple Press, Inc.

Tourists: © www.comstock.com.

Umatilla Black Bear Festival: Courtesy Florida Fish and Wildlife Commission.

Union Blockade: Florida State Archives.

Universities: Photo of UF arch © 1997 by Karelisa Hartigan, from *Guide to UF and Gainesville* by Kevin McCarthy and Murray D. Laurie © 1997. FSU façade photo by Murray D. Laurie, from *Guide to FSU & Tallahassee* by Murray D. Laurie © 1999. Both published by Pineapple Press, Inc.

Vegetables: All photos by U.S. Department of Agriculture, Agricultural Research Service.

Venice: Shark's tooth photo by Robin Brown.

Vizcaya: Vizcaya and James Deering photos courtesy Vizcaya Museum and Gardens.

Volusia County: Jeans photo by June Cussen.

Vulture: David Nellis.

Walt Disney World: Cinderella castle photo © Disney Enterprises. Used by permission.

Watermelons: U.S. Department of Agriculture, Agricultural Research Service.

Weedon Island: Photo courtesy Florida Museum of Natural History. Pottery illustrations by Robin Brown.

Wells, Williams Charles: Florida State Archives.

Wood Stork: Photo by Charles Caniff, from *Common Coastal Birds of Florida and the Caribbean* by David Nellis © 2001. Published by Pineapple Press, Inc.

Worm Grunting: Florida State Archives.

Xeric Oak Scrub: Nancy D. Deyrup. Courtesy Archbold Biological Station.

Ximenez-Fatio House: Color photos courtesy The National Society of the Colonial Dames of America in the State of Florida. Illustration by H. Patrick Reed and Nan E. Wilson, from *Historic Homes of Florida* by Laura Stewart and Susanne Hupp © 1995. Published by Pineapple Press, Inc.

Loxahatchee National Wildlife Refuge: Susan D. Jewell.

Yankeetown: Florida State Archives.

Ybor City: Cigar shop photo, VISIT FLORIDA. Vicente Martinez-Ybor portrait, Florida State Archives.

Yellow-crowned Night Heron: Photo by David Nellis, from *Common Coastal Birds of Florida and the Caribbean* by David Nellis © 2001. Published by Pineapple Press, Inc.

Youth (Fountain of): Florida State Archives.

Yulee, David Levy: Florida State Archives.

Zebra Longwing: Peter Stiling.

Zellwood Sweet Corn Festival: Illustration by Carol Tornatore based on original photo by Zellwood Sweet Corn Festival.

Zephyrhills: Historic photo of Zephyrhills, Florida State Archives. Photo of Zephyrhills brand water bottle, June Cussen. Zephyrhills logo shown by permission of The Perrier Group of America.

Zoos: Animal images © 2002-2003 www.clipart.com.

Zora Neale Hurston: Library of Congress, American Folklife Center Collection.

Zorayda Castle: Courtesy St. Johns County Visitors & Conventions Bureau.

IF YOU ENJOYED READING THIS BOOK, here are some other books from Pineapple Press on related topics. Ask your local bookseller for our books. For a complete catalog, write to Pineapple Press, P.O. Box 3889, Sarasota, FL 34230 or call 1-800-PINEAPL (746-3275). Or visit our website at www.pineapplepress.com.

Drawing Florida Wildlife by Frank Lohan. The clearest, easiest method yet for learning to draw Florida's birds, reptiles, amphibians, and mammals. For all ages. ISBN 1-56164-090-5 (pb)

Esmeralda and the Enchanted Pond by Susan Ryan and Sandra Cook. Esmeralda and her dad visit a pond deep in a Florida forest. Her dad uses his imagination to explain the nature there, but Esmeralda wants to know the real reasons for what she sees. For ages 7–10. ISBN 1-56164-236-3 (hb)

The Florida Water Story by Peggy Lantz and Wendy Hale. Illustrates and describes many of the plants and animals that depend on the springs, rivers, beaches, marshes, and reefs in and around Florida, including corals, sharks, lobsters, alligators, manatees, birds, and turtles. For ages 10–14. ISBN 1-56164-099-9 (hb)

Legends of the Seminoles by Betty Mae Jumper. Illustrations by Guy LaBree. Meet mischievous Rabbit, the Corn Lady, the Deer Girl, and many other characters from these tales meant to teach young Seminoles the ways of life. For all ages. ISBN 1-56164-033-6 (hb) and ISBN 1-56164-040-9 (pb)

Sinkholes by Sandra Friend. What on earth is a sinkhole? There are lots of them in Florida, and they are much more than just places where the ground caved in. Learn all about why this happens. For ages 12 and up. ISBN 1-56164-258-4 (hb)

The Young Naturalist's Guide to Florida by Peggy Lantz and Wendy Hale. Plants, birds, insects, reptiles, and mammals are all around us. This enticing book shows you where and how to look for Florida's most interesting natural features and creatures. For ages 10–14. ISBN 1-56164-051-4 (pb)

Southern Fossil Discoveries Series
Three volumes by Judy Cutchins and Ginny Johnston loaded with full-color photos and original artwork. For ages 8–12:

Ice Age Giants of the South. Learn how prehistoric animals looked, how they lived, and what they ate. Includes full-color photos of fossil bones, reconstructed skeletons, and lifelike models of extinct creatures. ISBN 1-56164-195-2 (hb)

Giant Predators of the Ancient Seas. Discover how scientists use fossil clues to learn about the lives and habitats of the most exciting sea animals that ever lived. ISBN 1-56164-237-1 (hb)

Dinosaurs of the South. Every fossil uncovered presents new information about life in this region of North America during the time of the dinosaurs. Scientists have identified some entirely new dinosaur species known only in the South. ISBN 1-56164-266-5 (hb)

Pineapple Press Biographies for Young Readers Series
Introducing Floridians who have made a difference:

Gift of the Unicorn: The Story of Lue Gim Gong, Florida's Citrus Wizard by Virginia Aronson. Lue Gim Gong left his native China and sailed to the United States in 1872 at the age of 12. Thus began his lifelong journey of discovery and experimentation with citrus. For ages 9–12. ISBN 1-56164-264-9 (hb)

Konnichiwa Florida Moon: The Story of George Morikami, Pineapple Pioneer by Virginia Aronson. Meet Sukeji "George" Morikami, who arrived at the Japanese farming colony of Yamato in south Florida in 1906. Though he amassed a fortune through the sale of his pineapples, George remained a humble man throughout his life. His property is now the Morikami Museum and Japanese Gardens. For ages 7–10. ISBN 1-56164-263-0 (hb)